Contents

ISBN 978-1-84631-879-5

First published 2012 by
Liverpool University Press
4 Cambridge Street
Liverpool L69 7ZU

and

Liverpool City Council
Municipal Buildings
Dale St
Liverpool L2 2DH

British Library cataloguing-in-publication information

A British Library CIP record is available for this title

Printed and bound in the UK by Henry Ling Ltd

Foreword

Jean-Luc Courcoult, Artistic Director of Royal De Luxe, met me on a rainy day in June 2010 to talk me through what was to become one of the highlights of my leadership of the city council. He brought with him a passion, a story and an obsession associated with all great artists to make a difference.

We talked about north Liverpool and the obstacles and opportunities it faced, we talked about the area's connections with the *Titanic* story and we talked about our passion for engaging communities at all levels whether through art or through regeneration. He and I wanted this great work not just to feature our renowned city centre but to showcase parts of Liverpool which may not be as well-known to those outside the city but where there is real beauty and passionate people ready to make things happen.

And that is where the story begins.

Early in the planning stages it was estimated that crowds of around 250,000 would enjoy the event and the 800,000 turnout far exceeded expectations. Liverpool welcomed local, national and international visitors, all of whom were wowed not only by the story unfolding before their eyes but by the atmosphere and spirit of the people of Liverpool and the beauty of the city itself.

A staggering £32 million was generated for the local economy and as a result Sea Odyssey has been hailed the most successful cultural event Liverpool has ever staged. But this is not just an event that made sense economically. This story was inspired by Liverpool. I knew it would

capture the imagination of Liverpool people and become part of the collective memory, as everyone would engage with and embrace a story which, at its heart, was of human endeavour and love.

These are stories we should never ignore, because not only do they put into reality a city's ambition, but they transform a space so it's not just about bricks and mortar, but about humanity.

For three days in April this city was transformed and we engaged in a conversation about a little girl, her uncle, and her pet dog and the fourth character in this fairy tale – the city of Liverpool and her people.

I'm proud to be Mayor of a city which thinks big in everything it does. Sea Odyssey has set the benchmark for cultural events, not only in Liverpool but across the UK and Europe.

But Sea Odyssey is only the beginning of the next chapter in Liverpool's story, my ambition for this city is boundless.

I hope you enjoy this wonderful book and the memories it will bring, helping you re-live the weekend this city came together as one to give a warm Liverpool welcome to our very special giant guests.

Joe Anderson, OBE
Mayor of Liverpool

Titanic and Liverpool

Without a doubt, Sea Odyssey was a landmark event for Liverpool, fulfilling a promise to commemorate the centenary of the sinking of the *Titanic* in a sensitive and unforgettable manner.

Liverpool is one of seven Titanic Cities, along with Belfast, Cherbourg, Cobh (Co. Cork), Halifax (Nova Scotia), New York and Southampton, having strong and direct connections with the ill-fated liner.

Although the *Titanic* never came to the city, it was built as a result of Liverpool's position as a major world port, and was registered in the head office of the White Star Line, making Liverpool its home port.

The iconic Grade II* listed building, known as Albion House, still stands on the corner of James Street and serves as a poignant and constant reminder of the loss people suffered – particularly since this was where relatives flocked to hear news of whether their loved ones had survived the disaster.

And the connections between the *Titanic* and this great city continue.

At least 90 members of her crew were from Merseyside or had close links with the region. The lower deck corridor which ran the length of the ship was commonly known as 'Scotland Road' as a nod to the famous Liverpool thoroughfare of the same name. Captain Smith of the *Titanic* had himself been based on Merseyside for 40 years, before moving to Southampton in 1908.

The eight musicians in the *Titanic*'s band were recruited by music agents CW and FN Black of 14 Castle Street, Liverpool. There is much speculation about whether the musicians continued to play as the ship began to sink, but many feel they did, believing they performed 'Nearer, My God, To Thee' in those final, tragic moments.

The *Titanic*'s lookout who first spotted the iceberg was Fred Fleet, a Liverpudlian who survived the sinking but was said to be one of the final victims of the tragedy, as, tortured by the loss of so many lives, he committed suicide some years later.

The links between Liverpool and the *Titanic* are undeniably extensive. With so much history between the two, there was a vast amount to take into consideration

The R.M.S. "*TITANIC*," which Foundered on her Maiden Voyage to New York, April 15th, 1912.

SEA ODYSSEY
GIANT
SPECTACULAR
1912 2012

in the footsteps of GIANTS

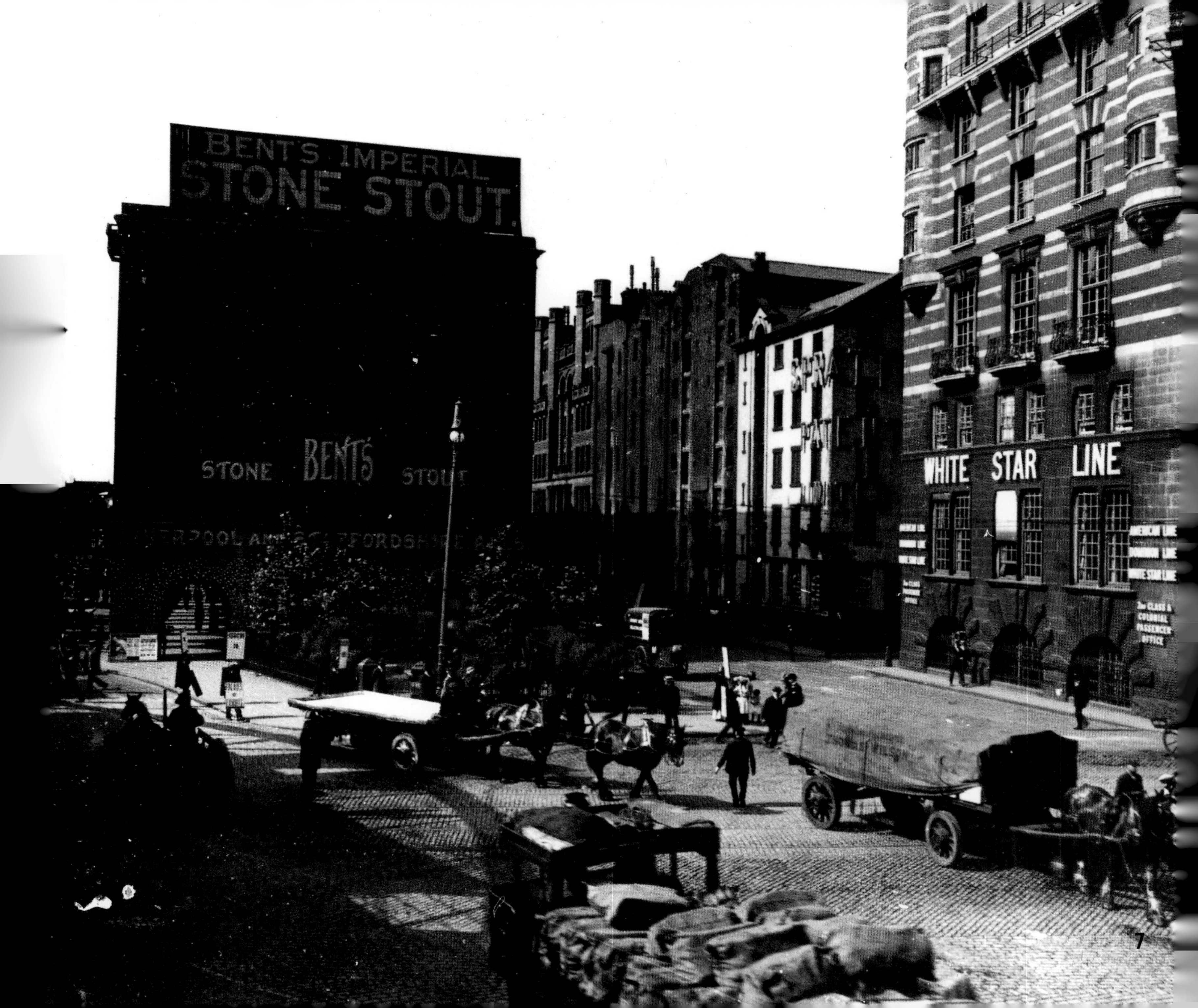
BENT'S IMPERIAL
STONE STOUT.
STONE BENT'S STOUT
WHITE STAR LINE
AMERICAN LINE
DOMINION LINE
WHITE STAR LINE
2nd CLASS &
COLONIAL
PASSENGER
OFFICE

DX/1013/R
1989/192

60 Empress Road
Kensington
Liverpool
13.4.12

Dear Father
It seems ages since I last seen you. I wish we where in Southampton with you it is very lonely without you Dear Father I have not been so very well I have had a a bad throat hoping I will soon get better for Mama worries so much little Ernie as not been so well but he as got better now hoping you are keeping well dada so ta love from Ivy and and Ernie thank dada for the presents love from all dada hoping to see you soon with love from Ivy and Mam and Ernie xxxxxxxxxx hisses for dada x

Dada this is my first letter

LOCAL MEMBERS OF TITANIC'S CREW.

LDP 20/4/1912 p 9

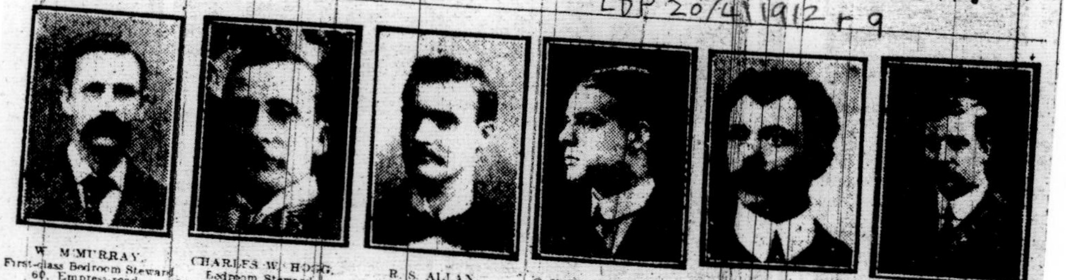

W. M'MURRAY, First-class Bedroom Steward, 60, Empress-road [Pettingell.

CHARLES W. HOGG, Bedroom Steward, 24, Bulwer-street, Everton. [Halls Studios, N.W.

R. S. ALLAN, Bedroom Steward, 70, Menzies-street, Dingle. [Medrington's.

C. F. W. SEDGWICK, St Helens.

JOHN ROBERT GILES, Second Baker, 28, Compton-street.

HENRY W. ASHE, Steward, 15, Wytesdale-road, Aintree.

when planning an event which would do justice to one of the most significant maritime disasters and pay respects to the families affected.

But one, seemingly untold story, struck a chord with the street theatre legends Royal de Luxe.

It was the story of a little girl and a heart-breaking letter which never reached its intended recipient.

Ten-year-old May McMurray lived at 60 Empress Road in Kensington, Liverpool. Longing to hear from her absent father William, on 13th April 1912 May put pen to paper for what would be her first ever letter. 'Dada' was a first-class bedroom steward on board the *Titanic*, but sadly, having sailed out of Southampton on the 10th of April, he never received his daughter's loving words. The news of William's death reached his wife Clara on 17th April 1912, their wedding anniversary.

Artistic Director of Royal de Luxe, Jean-Luc Courcoult, first came across this moving piece of history in the Merseyside Maritime Museum archives, and this small,

yet undeniably important story resonated with his creative imagination.

But how could a tale starring three Giants who explored the city be an appropriate expression of the importance of the *Titanic* to this city? After all, it was essential never to forget the fact that not only was the sinking of the ship a major world event, it was a tragic and bitter blow to the port and the people of Liverpool.

And herein lies just why this event surpassed everyone's expectations.

Sea Odyssey was not an event solely focused on the sinking of the *Titanic*. It was the story of the love between a father and a daughter which transcended time.

Inspired by young May's experience, these characters took to the city streets and, in front of hundreds of thousands of awe-struck spectators, created a story of love, loss and reunion in a three-day emotional rollercoaster ride.

The reference to the city's connection with the *Titanic* was subtle but constant.

Without a doubt, this was an occasion which marked the centenary of the maritime disaster, but as is typical of Liverpool, this city looked for a unique perspective, one that would engage, compel and stay with people for many years to come.

It was the human story of the *Titanic*. It was poignant, it was unforgettable. It was Liverpool.

Sarah Langworthy

ST. GEORGE'S HALL

MONDAY, MAY 20th, 1912, at 7-30

GRAND

VARIETY ◦◦ ENTERTAINMENT

IN AID OF THE

"TITANIC" DISASTER FUND.

Organised and arranged by the COMMANDER, OFFICERS and CREW of the WHITE STAR LINE, R.M.S. "BALTIC"; assisted by the COMMITTEE of the LIVERPOOL THEATRICAL GALA

Liverpool's 21st Century Cultural Renaissance

For me, as the Director of Culture Liverpool, the excitement began to build back in 2006 when talks began with Royal de Luxe.

I clearly remember meeting some of the team, seeing these beautiful, hand-drawn pictures of a deep sea diver and hearing for the first time the beginnings of a very different *Titanic* story with Liverpool at its heart.

I heard the full story five years later in May 2011 and it brought me to tears. However, I'm not ashamed to say this would not be the only time I cried over the next year. For me one of the reasons that great art works is that it brings emotions to the surface that under normal, everyday circumstances, you can control.

Fast-forward a year, and very early on a Friday morning my heart is in my mouth as I watch a 15,000-strong crowd in Stanley Park chanting 'Wake her up, wake her up'. The sun is fighting its way through the clouds, seemingly determined to shine on the welcome visitors who had invaded the park and our lives.

The wait seems interminable, but then the Little Girl Giant opens her eyes.

The gasps and exclamations from the audience say it all. This is magical and it feels like a privilege to be part of something which will journey not only through the city streets but though our hearts as well.

As I walked around the city for the next three days it was not only the unforgettable giant story unfolding in front of me, but also an amazing story of Liverpool being told all around me: children and their parents excitedly following every move, builders in their fluorescent jackets leaning through crowds of people in order to stroke the mischievous Xolo, elderly day care centre residents wrapped in blankets cheering the spectacle in front of them, and groups of young lads clambering up on a Portakabin to get the best view at Everton Park.

No other city embraces these kinds of events like Liverpool. In our eyes, the giants were real, and they touched every single person who felt a genuine connection to them and to the moving story which was played out in such a beautiful, poignant way.

I think what makes this event even more special is that ten years ago we could only have dreamed about putting on an event of this calibre and scale. At this time Liverpool aspired to be a premier European city, but in many ways it fell short of the aspiration.

It had culture, it had heritage, it had passion, it had huge potential. All it needed was a catalyst.

And this catalyst came in the shape of the bid to become European Capital of Culture in 2008 – this was our moment to shine and show the world exactly what Liverpool was made of.

A programme was developed which put culture at the heart of everything, using it as a springboard to rejuvenate and redevelop the city.

More than £4 billion was invested in the physical transformation of the city. Areas which were beginning to look tired were brought back to life to reach their full potential, with the creation of developments including Liverpool ONE, the Echo Arena and BT Convention Centre, and the opening of the Liverpool Cruise Terminal. And let's not forget that some of the city's best-loved gems also benefited from extensive renovations, including St George's Hall, the Bluecoat and World Museum Liverpool.

The unprecedented collaboration of the public and private sector made it possible for us to achieve a common goal and resulted in us breaking all previous records, with 15 million cultural visits and an overall economic impact that saw £800 million brought into the region in 2008 alone.

And, of course, these figures, while outstanding and speaking for themselves in terms of how successful the year was, do not tell the whole story. For me, the real success was the reaction of people not only in Liverpool but across the world.

The Capital of Culture title changed perceptions of the city. Liverpool was an unrivalled stage where we demonstrated the amazing diversity of high art, big outdoor free events and provocative new theatre.

The journey of 2008 began on a high with the People's Opening, and the bar was raised throughout the rest of that momentous year. Even today, just the mention of Paul McCartney at Liverpool Sound, the Shankly Show, *King Lear*, Klimt at Tate Liverpool, the MTV Music Awards, the Tall Ships Races and Go Superlambananas elicits an enthusiastic and passionate response. And then of course you could talk about a 50-foot mechanical spider which explored the city's streets, a 2008 highlight for many and, unbeknown at the time, a delightful taster of what to expect four years on!

Imaginations were captured, hearts were won.

It was declared 'one of the most successful Capital of Culture programmes' by the President of the European Commission, José Manuel Barroso.

And as 2008 ended on an emotional high, we wanted the message to be loud and clear: Liverpool has a unique cultural offer and we, with cultural partners across the city, would do all we could to celebrate, promote and build on the momentum created by the year.

As a result this city has not rested on its laurels. We have continued to host high quality events, with internationally renowned brands such as MOBO approaching us to host their shows, which are viewed by audiences world-wide.

Born out of Go Superlambananas and Go Penguins, Liverpool Discovers had thousands of people exploring the city to enjoy extraordinary pieces of art. And, building on the immense regeneration witnessed, there has been a recent addition unveiled on the Waterfront. The Museum of Liverpool, a £78 million venue, is the world's first national museum completely devoted to the history of a city.

Liverpool's importance as a tourist destination has taken another step forward with the Liverpool Cruise Terminal being given turnaround status, meaning that this city, with its long and proud maritime heritage, can embark passengers on liners beginning and ending their cruises in the heart of the city centre.

Since 2008, the city's reputation for putting on unmissable, free outdoor events has gone from strength to strength. Marking the centenary of one of the city's most enduring symbols, the Liver Building, a mind-blowing 3D *son et lumière* display brought the building to life, creating a digital homage to Liverpool's history.

And there is the sense that everything was leading up to April 2012, when Sea Odyssey brought so much joy to the city.

There are very few cities in the world, let alone in this country, fortunate enough to work with the creative *tour de force* that is Royal de Luxe. But we know Liverpool is somewhere very special.

The architecture and historical nature of our buildings are the perfect stage setting for any performance, and one of the many lessons we learned from 2008 was that we should fully exploit our existing cultural assets, particularly when many of those assets are unrivalled throughout the country.

I think we all felt a degree of sadness when, on a blustery, grey Sunday afternoon, our three new giant friends sailed away on the River Mersey to continue their adventures.

The aftermath of Sea Odyssey was quite simple. In terms of culture, the city would never be the same again.

We always knew what the city could achieve. We knew it could put on a breathtaking show that would go down in the city's history as one of its most awe-inspiring events. And now the whole world knows exactly what Liverpool can do.

What comes next?

This city is open to artists and creatives that draw on the beauty of this city. It has the most incredible stage and story to play with. Sea Odyssey is just the beginning.

Claire McColgan, MBE
Director of Culture Liverpool

Royal de Luxe:
A Phenomenon in Street Theatre

Over the past three decades, Royal de Luxe has become a legendary street theatre company. Founded in 1979, they are known not just for breathing life into giants, but for a practice that extends over a wide range of different forms of street theatre.

This short summary of their work provides a glimpse into the world of this exceptional troupe of actors, aerialists, engineers, metal-workers and inventors, all poets in their trade. Many of the qualities and characteristics of Royal de Luxe's creations and methods of working resonate with Liverpool, itself a legendary, global port city, and this strengthened the way in which the local audience responded to Sea Odyssey.

Jean-Luc Courcoult: The Early Days

As a boy, Jean-Luc Courcoult's interest in photography came before his passion for theatre, and this love of photography continues today as the power of the image is a motor for his work. He discovered theatre as a method for communicating with the world at the age of 14, and enrolled in theatre school. His very first creations were in collaboration with fellow artists from this school. Jean-Luc continued acting in his productions until 1984, from which time he focused on directing.

The name of the company was a projection of everything they were not, a grand name tinged with irony for a troupe of then penniless street performers. However, there is also an unexpected and very practical reason for their name, in that it referred to the name of the rolls of tape upon which they wrote their first plays: chosen because they split into multiple segments, allowing for several different narratives to be developed simultaneously.

After their first show in Aix-en-Provence, Royal de Luxe established their base in the picturesque Cévennes in South West France from where they produced numerous touring shows, including The Blessing of the Cours Mirabeau by the Pope, Terror in the Elevator, Shoe Parking and The Semi-Final of Waterclash.

In 1984 the company moved to a ruined castle near Toulouse with luxurious grounds within which to play and create. In 1987 their first major touring show, which became known as Photo Novel, was launched and went on to tour twenty-two European, Latin American and African countries as well as Australia and New Zealand, Canada and Russia up until 1991.

Enduring Principles

A few strong and simple principles established by these early shows have endured over the decades, affording Royal de Luxe their inimitable style and reputation. Crucially, all of their shows are free to the public and happen outdoors. The company is very protective of both the images they create and the context in which they are revealed, which maintains a suspension of disbelief and increases the public's sense

of awe and wonder. From the inception of Royal de Luxe, familiar daily objects and scrap have been used to compose surprising dreamlike scenarios with expertly engineered machines, and magic is found in the very visible human interaction with these objects. As Odile Quirot writes in her introduction to the anthology of Royal de Luxe creations from 1993 to 2001:

> 'Royal de Luxe are reviving the world of childhood in theatre, which seems to be both funny and serious, magic and crafted.'[1]

Quirot points out that the work encourages people to openly express their natural reactions to the extraordinary tale unfolding before their eyes. Music has also become a signature element of Royal de Luxe's shows, lending a dynamic and haunting power to the images Jean-Luc creates.

Move to Nantes

1989 saw the closure of the last shipyard in Nantes, leaving the city at a low point economically and in terms of morale. At the same time Jean-Luc Courcoult was tiring of working in the South West. He had an idea that Royal de Luxe should be based on a ship and started to scour French ports. Jean-Marc Ayrault, Mayor of Nantes (who was later to become Prime Minister of France in 2012), was quick to see the win-win opportunity and, by offering Royal de Luxe a workshop space to build and rehearse their creations, Monsieur Ayrault played an instrumental role in brokering the love affair between the company and the people of Nantes – which endures to this day.

A Preoccupation with Port Cities

Nantes, like Liverpool, is a celebrated port city, the place from where author Jules Verne watched adventurers leave to explore the world. Jean-Luc Courcoult's move to Nantes gave him a base from which to realise his dream of the company touring the world by boat.

The operation Cargo 92, commissioned as part of the commemoration of the 500th anniversary of the discovery of America, became the vehicle for this. Royal de Luxe converted the hold of an immense cargo ship into a French city street and toured Latin America with their show The True History of France together with members of the Philippe Découflé dance company, Mano Negra band and Philippe Genty puppet company. The work was showcased in Caracas (Venezuela), Bogotá and Cartagena (Colombia), Santo Domingo (Dominican Republic), Rio and São Paulo (Brazil), Montevideo (Uruguay) and Buenos Aires (Argentina).

Royal de Luxe broke the mould with this act, which was a world away from a traditional street theatre show.

Global Reach and Invention of New Forms

Royal de Luxe rarely stopped moving in their infancy. They toured Moroccan villages and markets, and followed this with residencies in rural Cameroon and China. These visits opened the company's eyes and minds to new and different cultural belief systems and lifestyles, strongly influencing their practice. Jean-Luc Courcoult explains his purpose in taking the company to these remote areas:

---

1   *Royal de Luxe 1993–2001: Entretiens avec Jean-Luc Courcoult realisés par Olde Quirot et Michel Loulergue* (Arles: Actes Sud, 2001), p. 18.

'To find a place where you don't feel at home and to get by with materials which you can get hold of, to question yourself and to create.'

When Jean-Luc creates something new, he starts from zero and allows the subconscious to bring in the elements of what resonates with that particular place, recognising the reference points of the audience there.

In Cameroon, the initial way of writing on rolls of tape resurfaced as Royal de Luxe devised a form of theatre with multiple narratives, never knowing in advance which would play out. Jean-Luc reflects how this form mirrored the company's experience of the African continent:

'If I had wanted to create an ordinary structure for "Little Negro Tales, working title", I could have done… But to put on a show which can take off in any direction presents a real challenge. For me, it is this discovery of a different structure which represents our difficulties in understanding Africa.'

The Giants' Saga

Inspiration came to Jean-Luc when he was gazing out of a plane window on his way to Rio and was captivated by the sweeping vistas of the famous city, with its breathtaking mountains dominating the landscape. Jean-Luc's mind wandered to the legend of the sleeping giant that lies under the Pão de Açúcar Mountain in Rio de Janeiro. It was then that his ambition was conceived to create a giant whose sheer scale would inspire the same sense of awe and wonder.

The Giant was born in the port city of Le Havre, where initial extracts from his dreams and nightmares started appearing in the street like a cacophony of happenings, and finally the sleeping Giant awoke. This Giant would later evolve into the magnificent Diver, who wowed the Liverpool crowds.

In Liverpool, the Lilliputians (the amazing workers who manoeuvre the giants) were reminded of their experience at Le Havre, especially in the reactions, belief and joyous participation from the crowds in the city.

From Le Havre the Giants have travelled the world, never growing old, carrying with them the experience of significant events in world history, such as the 20th anniversary of the fall of the Berlin Wall and the centenary of the Mexican Revolution. The combination of the meaning of such events in the collective consciousness, the architecture which becomes the set, and the spirit of cities, inspires new voyages.

As well as three gigantic time-travellers in human form, the company has created a giant rhinoceros, two giraffes, the Sultan's Elephant and, most recently, the Mexican dog, Xolo.

Jean-Luc explains the importance of the life-giving Lilliputians:

'The operators have to live every moment of the action. They are nothing without the giraffe and, without them, the giraffe does not exist. Their presence in the field of vision is helpful because they provide the human aspect of the animal.'

In Liverpool, the pure human effort and transparent working of the machines certainly increased the engagement with the crowds.

To Jean-Luc the Giants represent real-life characters. He said when talking about the Little Girl Giant:

'I simply believe that she is real… Once we achieve a level of reality…we have found something strange which is at once true and untrue, and it makes you really want to believe.'

One week before the show in Liverpool, Jean-Luc reflected fondly on the time when Etienne Louvieaux, the creator of special effects, leant over a bar in Reykjavík and casually suggested creating a 25-metre-high geyser to announce the arrival of the Giants. Jean-Luc belly-laughs as he remembers the absurdity coupled with the brilliance of this imaginative suggestion. Hence it has become part of Royal de Luxe's mythology that movements of tectonic plates, triggered by the Giants' arrival, trigger natural geysers.

The year in which the Little Girl Giant visited London, Jean-Luc came to Liverpool to research a possible show for 2008, and this is when the idea of creating a Diver character came to him. It therefore seemed poetic and correct that the Diver and the Little Girl Giant should come home to Liverpool, hence the title Sea Odyssey. Revisiting the city some years later, Jean-Luc read once again the poignant letter from May McMurray to her father, which added a strong dimension of 'imaginary realism' to the myth which played out across the city.

And straight from Liverpool, Royal de Luxe went on to premiere and tour a new show, Fall Street, which dramatises and explodes the cinematic form of the Western.

You can guarantee that whatever is around the corner will be just as unexpected!

For more information on the company, visit **www.royal-de-luxe.com**

Polly Moseley

Sea Odyssey

The Sea of Liverpool has swallowed up so many sailors, travellers and adventurers that you would think it was a cannibal.

Icebergs are boat hunters and Liverpudlians huge children with eyes full of hope and rebellion.

For the unsinkable *Titanic*, her first voyage was also to be her last. But let's move right away to the story of one stowaway: loaded on board during the night, unnoticed – a thirty-foot-tall Giant, capable of travelling through time, on his way to another continent to meet his daughter, the Little Giant.

Giants don't grow old, don't grow up, they just stay the age they are for eternity – that is, if they don't die.

Disaster struck in the Atlantic Ocean; everyone knows the details of the accident. The ocean liner was the pride of Liverpool, and many different Liverpudlian tradesmen were recruited, mainly to maintain the ship and to look after the passengers.

But let's return to our gigantic passenger trapped in one of the holds. He feels the full force of the iceberg's blade. The sea rushes into the ship so fiercely that he is unable to move.

He is a prisoner and plummets 12,000 feet with the *Titanic*. We believe that, knowing he would soon die, he took his last underwater lift ride before coming to rest in a cloud of dust on the ocean bed. Above, petrified with fear, survivors hoped for miracles – some were rescued, that too is known.

When the Little Giant heard the news, she sought out her uncle, the Great Giant's brother. While listening to her, the uncle made a decision that was to take him a century to carry out.

First, he would make himself a diving suit. Then he would scour the ocean floor for the shipwreck. After that, he would bury his brother in the deep-sea bed. Most importantly, he would come back with the letter the Great Giant had written to the Little Girl Giant. This is why he walked for many long years across the ocean floor, pulling the *Titanic*'s mail trunk to bring back the post to Liverpool.

Such tragedies do not affect the Little Giant's morale, who bravely decided to come to the reunion.

While reading magazines before leaving, she discovered that there are another two famed legends in Liverpool – the music of the Beatles, and the sheer passion for football of the rebel city.

Before setting up her first camp in Stanley Park, between the two football stadiums north of the city, she decides she will go on a cruise through the town on a road-sailing boat. A few hours before her arrival, as if by magic, a geyser shoots up from the ground in the city centre, to herald her arrival.

Written by Jean-Luc Courcoult
Author, Artistic Director and Founder
Royal de Luxe

Thursday 19th April 2012

Something strange was happening in the city.

A giant anchor appeared in King's Dock apparently out of nowhere. Had it been washed up? Or maybe beamed down? Visitors approached the unusual object with curiosity and just a little bit of trepidation. What did it mean?

Further down the waterfront, shocked screams could be heard. A giant geyser erupted in front of the Port of Liverpool building, soaking unsuspecting passers-by. A brave few stayed in the vicinity watching the impressive 50-foot water fountain, and the more mischievous bystanders encouraged others to take a closer look at the broken paving stones, feigning innocence about what was about to happen in just a few seconds time.

Experts declared something was disturbing the earth's tectonic plates. And whatever it was, it was big and heading for Liverpool...

Friday 20th April 2012

As the sun broke free of a cloudy Liverpool sky, it seemed like just another ordinary spring morning.

But it soon became clear that it was to be a day like no other. For stirring from her slumber in Stanley Park was a Little Girl Giant, on a quest to receive news about her father, a stowaway on the ill-fated *Titanic*.

So began Sea Odyssey, an extraordinary piece of street theatre which captured the hearts and imaginations of hundreds of thousands of people in Liverpool and beyond.

More than 15,000 people flocked to north Liverpool to witness the beginning of the magical tale. It was the first time an event of this scale had taken place in this part of the city. And the sight of the 30-foot giant and her dog Xolo striding majestically along Walton Lane and Vauxhall Road, taking in Anfield and Goodison stadiums, engendered a sense of pride in an area which has faced significant social challenges.

After taking a nap at Everton Brow, the Little Girl Giant headed for the waterfront, via the city centre. As she walked past St George's Hall and Lime Street Station, she was greeted by huge crowds, who were given affectionate licks by Xolo, with a few lucky schoolchildren being given rides by the effervescent canine. And as the sun set over Kings Dock, the Little Girl danced, before changing into her nightdress and climbing into her giant bed for the night.

Earlier, the 50-foot Uncle Giant, clad in diving suit, had emerged dramatically from the water at the Salthouse Dock. Crowds lined the dock perimeter, three- and four-deep, to see the appearance of the uncle, who was carrying a letter he had discovered on the ocean floor and kept with him for the past 100 years, written by the Little Girl Giant's father to his beloved daughter.

He walked past the former headquarters of the White Star Line, the owners of the *Titanic*, and had a historic meeting at the Town Hall with the Lord Mayor of Liverpool and guests, before ending the day's travels at Stanley Park, where the Little Girl's journey had begun that morning. There, he slept.

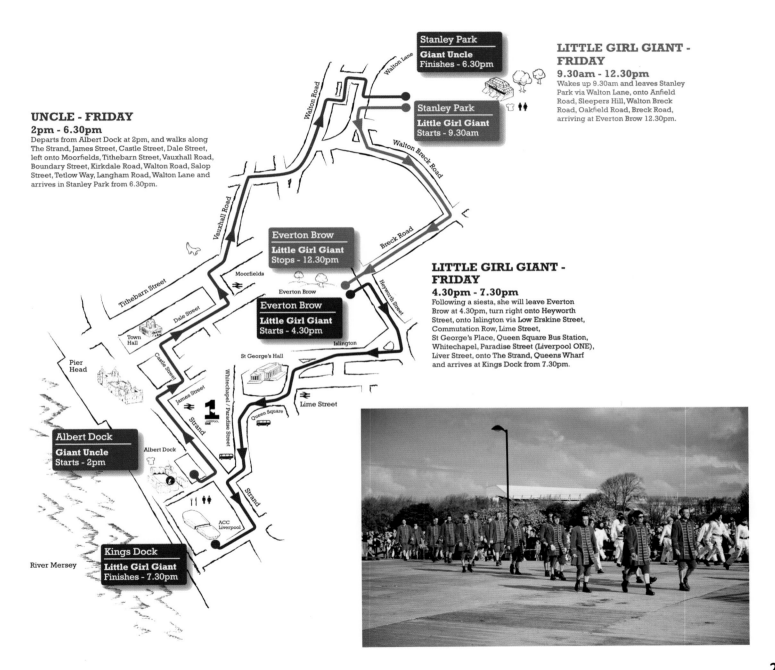

Stanley Park

Giant Uncle
Finishes - 6.30pm

Stanley Park

Little Girl Giant
Starts - 9.30am

LITTLE GIRL GIANT - FRIDAY

9.30am - 12.30pm

Wakes up 9.30am and leaves Stanley Park via Walton Lane, onto Anfield Road, Sleepers Hill, Walton Breck Road, Oakfield Road, Breck Road, arriving at Everton Brow 12.30pm.

UNCLE - FRIDAY

2pm - 6.30pm

Departs from Albert Dock at 2pm, and walks along The Strand, James Street, Castle Street, Dale Street, left onto Moorfields, Tithebarn Street, Vauxhall Road, Boundary Street, Kirkdale Road, Walton Road, Salop Street, Tetlow Way, Langham Road, Walton Lane and arrives in Stanley Park from 6.30pm.

Everton Brow

Little Girl Giant
Stops - 12.30pm

Everton Brow

Little Girl Giant
Starts - 4.30pm

LITTLE GIRL GIANT - FRIDAY

4.30pm - 7.30pm

Following a siesta, she will leave Everton Brow at 4.30pm, turn right onto Heyworth Street, onto Islington via Low Erskine Street, Commutation Row, Lime Street, St George's Place, Queen Square Bus Station, Whitechapel, Paradise Street (Liverpool ONE), Liver Street, onto The Strand, Queens Wharf and arrives at Kings Dock from 7.30pm.

Albert Dock

Giant Uncle
Starts - 2pm

Kings Dock

Little Girl Giant
Finishes - 7.30pm

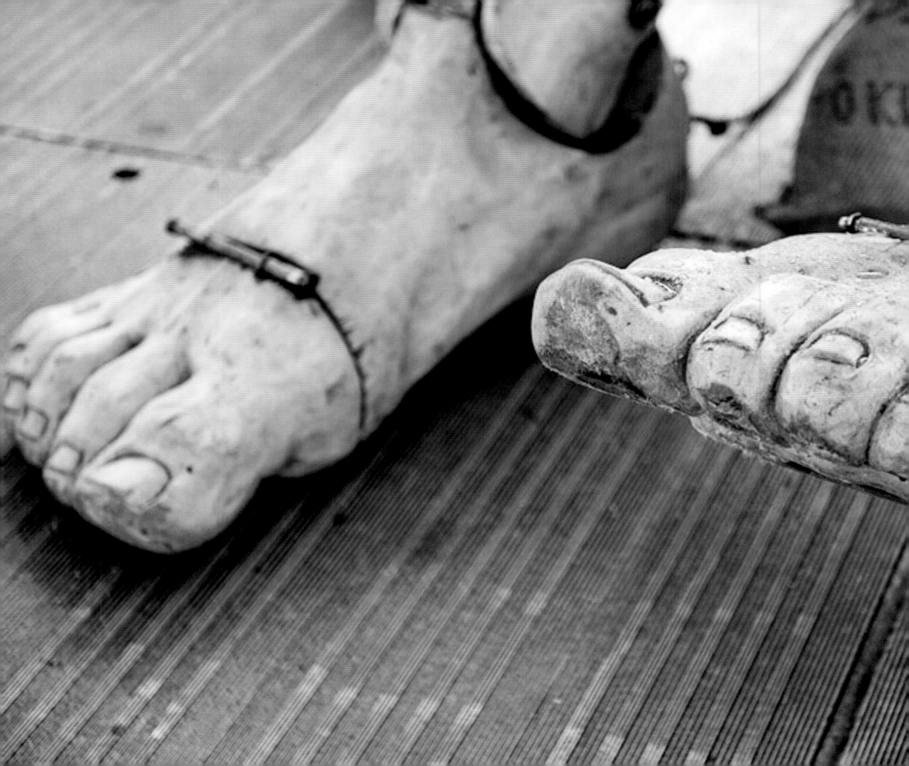

TITANIC
& LIVERPOOL
The untold story

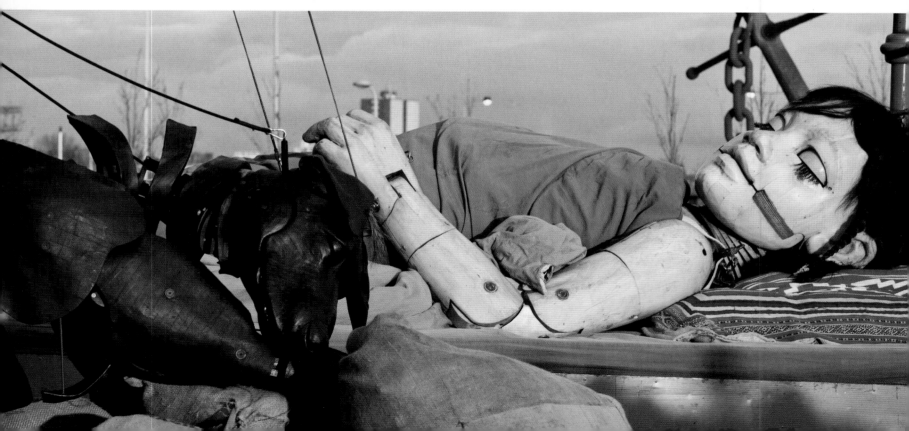

Saturday 21st April 2012

Saturday saw the Little Girl Giant awaken to crowds of 3,000 at Kings Dock and travel around Liverpool's business district, by boat, on foot and on a scooter, before taking a siesta in an enormous deckchair.

The Uncle Giant woke up in Stanley Park at 11am and followed a route into the city centre, passing Anfield stadium, accompanied by 'You'll Never Walk Alone', played by Royal de Luxe's live band.

Watched by 40,000 people, he snoozed at St George's Hall, before heading to St Luke's Church and continuing his journey by 'leaping' over the city's famous Chinese Arch.

At Kings Dock he removed his helmet, as if sensing his moment of destiny was about to arrive.

Then it happened: the Little Girl Giant appeared and the century-long search was over. There were few dry eyes among the crowds as girl and uncle came together in an embrace, staying that way as the sun set over the Mersey.

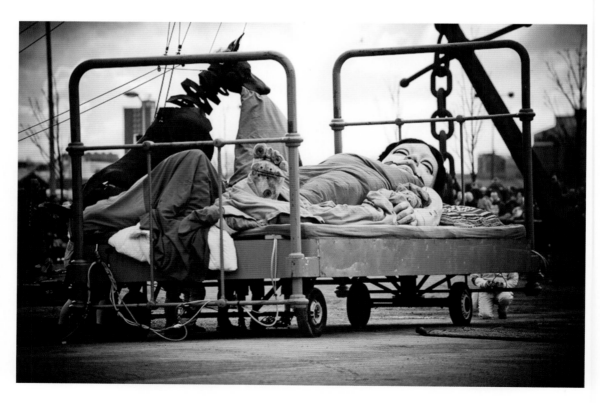

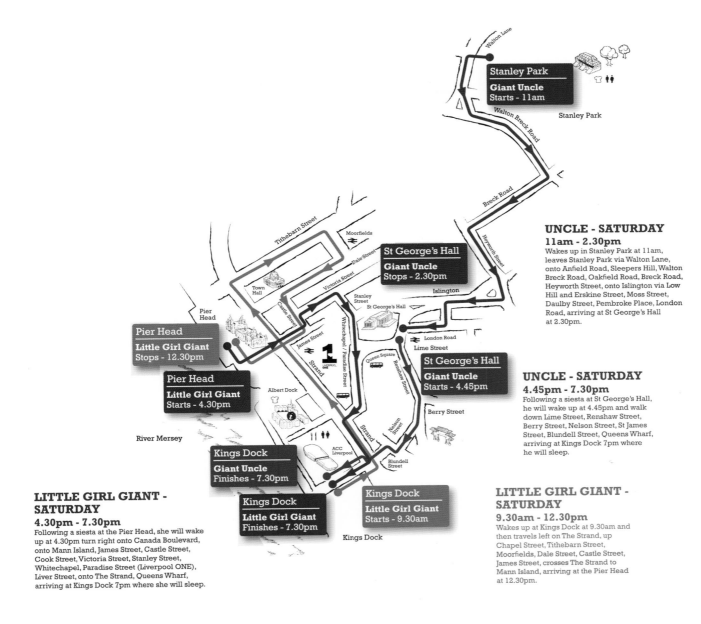

Stanley Park
Giant Uncle
Starts - 11am

Stanley Park

St George's Hall
Giant Uncle
Stops - 2.30pm

UNCLE - SATURDAY
11am - 2.30pm
Wakes up in Stanley Park at 11am, leaves Stanley Park via Walton Lane, onto Anfield Road, Sleepers Hill, Walton Breck Road, Oakfield Road, Breck Road, Heyworth Street, onto Islington via Low Hill and Erskine Street, Moss Street, Daulby Street, Pembroke Place, London Road, arriving at St George's Hall at 2.30pm.

Pier Head
Little Girl Giant
Stops - 12.30pm

Pier Head
Little Girl Giant
Starts - 4.30pm

St George's Hall
Giant Uncle
Starts - 4.45pm

UNCLE - SATURDAY
4.45pm - 7.30pm
Following a siesta at St George's Hall, he will wake up at 4.45pm and walk down Lime Street, Renshaw Street, Berry Street, Nelson Street, St James Street, Blundell Street, Queens Wharf, arriving at Kings Dock 7pm where he will sleep.

Kings Dock
Giant Uncle
Finishes - 7.30pm

Kings Dock
Little Girl Giant
Finishes - 7.30pm

Kings Dock
Little Girl Giant
Starts - 9.30am

LITTLE GIRL GIANT - SATURDAY
4.30pm - 7.30pm
Following a siesta at the Pier Head, she will wake up at 4.30pm turn right onto Canada Boulevard, onto Mann Island, James Street, Castle Street, Cook Street, Victoria Street, Stanley Street, Whitechapel, Paradise Street (Liverpool ONE), Liver Street, onto The Strand, Queens Wharf, arriving at Kings Dock 7pm where she will sleep.

LITTLE GIRL GIANT - SATURDAY
9.30am - 12.30pm
Wakes up at Kings Dock at 9.30am and then travels left on The Strand, up Chapel Street, Tithebarn Street, Moorfields, Dale Street, Castle Street, James Street, crosses The Strand to Mann Island, arriving at the Pier Head at 12.30pm.

Widnes (A561)

Liverpool

Wallasey
Birkenhead (Tunnels)
A5047

P 600 Queen Square

P 620 St John's Centre

Outer
Controlled
ZONE

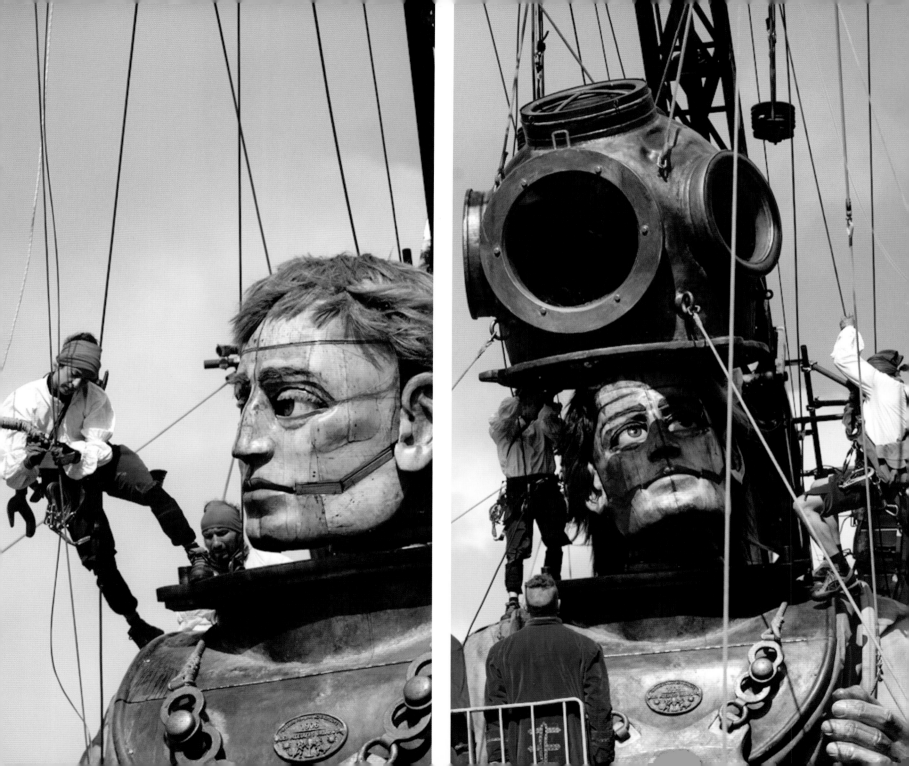

Sunday 22nd April 2012

The climax of Sea Odyssey arrived with the giants waking together on Sunday morning for the presentation of the long-lost letter. The Little Girl Giant danced in celebration and girl, uncle and dog paraded along the Strand. A huge cannon fired letters and postcards into the crowd, written by local people imagining they were on board the *Titanic*.

The giants waved goodbye to the Three Graces and were craned on to the boat *James Jackson Grundy*, before embarking on their final journey, out on to the Mersey, over the horizon and out of sight.

And then, it was over, and another important chapter in Liverpool's cultural story had been written.

Sea Odyssey was an extraordinary achievement for Liverpool, bringing home the human story of *Titanic* in a unique and poignant way.

But even more than that, it brought together people of all ages in a unified sense of wonder that would live on long after the giants' footsteps had faded from the city's streets.

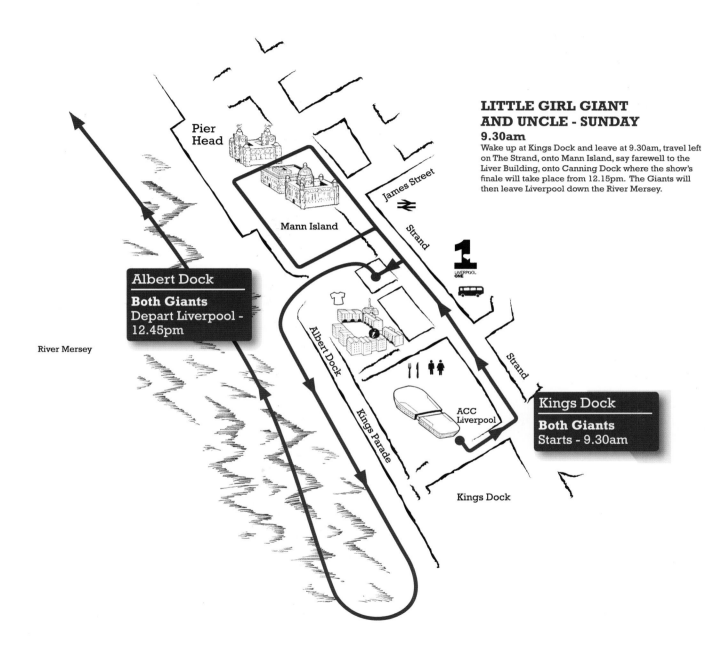

LITTLE GIRL GIANT
AND UNCLE - SUNDAY
9.30am
Wake up at Kings Dock and leave at 9.30am, travel left on The Strand, onto Mann Island, say farewell to the Liver Building, onto Canning Dock where the show's finale will take place from 12.15pm. The Giants will then leave Liverpool down the River Mersey.

Pier Head

Mann Island

James Street

Strand

LIVERPOOL ONE

Albert Dock

Both Giants
Depart Liverpool -
12.45pm

River Mersey

Albert Dock

Kings Parade

Strand

ACC Liverpool

Kings Dock

Both Giants
Starts - 9.30am

Kings Dock

Dear Scousers,

Before distributing the mail to the people of Liverpool, I will read to you the letter that the Great Giant sent to the Little Giant.

My Dearest Daughter,

Imagine that in the greatest secret and the dead of the night I embarked on board the Titanic – the Lilliputians did things well, by distracting the crew, whilst sneaking me into the hold and hiding me in the deepest part of the ship. I have to say that the Captain was in on it.

I'm comfortable, I don't need a thing, and the Lilliputians are looking after me. They built a huge cabin for me with suspended chandeliers, a mahogany bed and an enormous quilt. They extended the luxury into building a massive fireplace using pipes to deviate the smoke towards the ship's chimney.

The only downside is that, not having a porthole, I cannot see the sea. But I feel that with her big waves, the sea is taking me into her arms, as I hope to be able to hold you in mine.

Your Daddy, who's devouring you with love…

Acknowledgements

Sea Odyssey was produced by Liverpool City Council and we would like to thank all the staff across the council who worked tirelessly to bring this show to the streets of Liverpool.

We would also like to thank all the members of Royal de Luxe who travelled to Liverpool, the artistry and commitment they demonstrated were truly spectacular.

Finally, Liverpool City Council would also like to extend a massive thank you to all our partners, volunteers and the people of Liverpool whose support made this event such a tremendous success. The list of those we personally wish to thank is endless.

Letters and Stories

May McMurray letter reproduced with the permission of her family.

Sea Odyssey Story and Letter by Jean-Luc Courcoult, Royal de Luxe.

Titanic archive images provided by Liverpool Record Office, Liverpool Libraries.

Samples of the 100 letters written by Liverpool residents and schoolchildren which were fired from the cannon on the final day of the show – produced thanks to Liverpool schools, Writing on the Wall, Windows Project, North End Writers and Blackburne House.

Artwork

Giant Spectacular design concept by Black and Ginger.

On behalf of all who read this book a heartfelt thank you goes to all the photographers and their stunning images, without which this book would not exist.

Official Photographers

Ant Clausen (commissioned by Liverpool City Council)

New Zealand-born, self-taught photographer Ant Clausen started his professional career 30m underwater filming sharks in Australia and Egypt. Five years later, he is based in Liverpool, making the most of his love of photography by capturing people, places, events and local colour. From the Queen to Liverpool's Mathew Street Music Festival, Ant's laid-back approach effortlessly captures a look that says it all and infuses each image with a little 'Kiwi magic'. Recent work in Argentina for Condé Nast has broadened his photographic horizons and inspired him for future work abroad, but for now he is more than content to call Liverpool home.
www.photographyliverpool.com

Serge Koutchintsky (commissioned by Royal de Luxe)

Serge Koutchintsky was trained as a medical photographer and has been the professional photographer for Royal de Luxe since 2010, as well as collaborating with a wide range of well-known magazines. His philosophy is that environment is a way of thinking, and not just about nature. He has always had a passion for India and is mounting a series of global exhibitions on the Varanasi cremations, including a show in the renowned Paseo de la Reforma, Mexico City, during the annual 'month of death' in November 2012.
sergekoutchinsky@gmail.com

Mark McNulty
(commissioned by Liverpool City Council)

Mark McNulty's vast portfolio chronicles the people and culture of Liverpool since the late 1980s and offers a unique insight into the life of the city. His work, exhibited and published widely throughout the UK and on an international platform, is a blend of music, arts, events, advertising, fashion and portraiture that documents the city and its people. In 2008 his book *Pop Cultured* was published by Liverpool University Press, celebrating 20 years of music photography and featuring some of the biggest names in music. His regular Liverpool blog, recognised as a 'must read' by the *Guardian*, can be found at **www.rivercool.co.uk**, and his portfolio and archive can be viewed at **www.markmcnulty.co.uk**.

Contributing Photographers

Mederic Anfray, Stephen Bailey, Rebecca Barker, Richard Bell, Liam Birch, Anthony Bradshaw, Rachel Brockley, Peter Byrne, Ian Calcutt, Pete Carr, Deborah Chantler, Lorraine Cross, Samantha Cunningham, Andrew Dawson, Michael Fahy, Paul Gallagher, Glenn Hewitson, Paul Hughes, Shaun Jeffers, Kevin Johnston, Kevin Kelly, Chris Kerfoot, Annie Khanna, Jason Lanceley, Ian Lane, Michael Legg, Sally Lupton, Amy Maghill, Jude McLoughlin, Terry Mealey, Stéphan Ménoret, Nick Mercer, Mocha, Andrew Mitchell, Debra Moran, Susan Murphy, Kevin Newbold, Ian Nixon, Lindsay Panting, Sarah Roberts, Régis Routier, Barry Sarath, John Shirley, Christian Smith, Wesley Storey, Jemma Street, Martin Waters, Aaron Welsh, Stephen Whittaker.

Liverpool City Council and Royal de Luxe would like to extend a big thank you to all our funders and sponsors without whom this show would not have taken place.

it's liverpool